Inside Animals

Whales

and Other Mammals

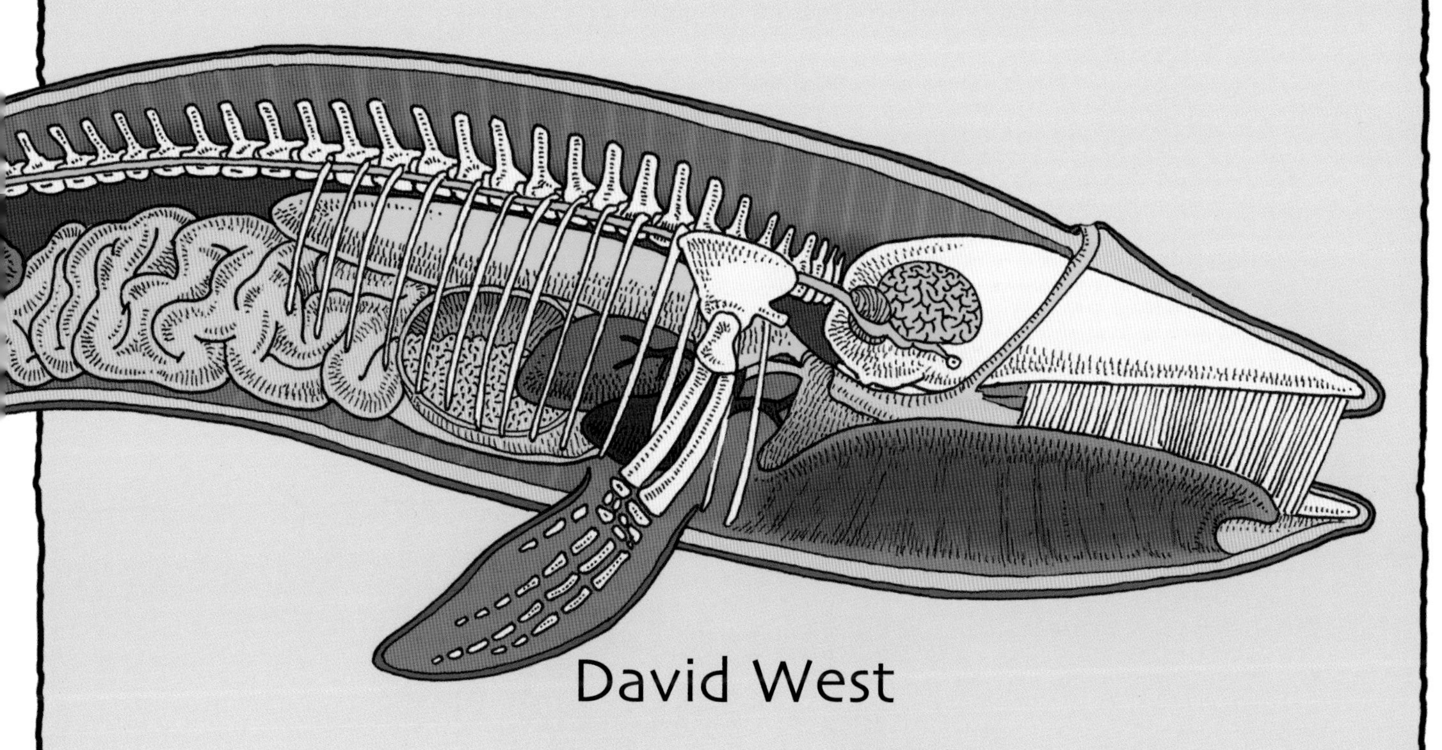

David West

WINDMILL BOOKS

Published in 2018 by **Windmill Books**,
an imprint of Rosen Publishing
29 East 21st Street, New York, NY 10010

Designed and illustrated *by* David West

CATALOGING-IN-PUBLICATION DATA
Names: West, David.
Title: Whales and other mammals / David West.
Description: New York : Windmill Books, 2018. | Series: Inside animals | Includes index.
Identifiers: ISBN 9781508194316 (pbk.) | ISBN 9781508193920 (library bound) | ISBN 9781508194378 (6 pack)
Subjects: LCSH: Whales–Juvenile literature. | Mammals–Juvenile literature.
Classification: LCC QL706.2 W47 2018 | DDC 599'.03–dc23

Manufactured in China
CPSIA Compliance Information: Batch BW18WM: For Further Information contact Rosen Publishing, New York, New York at 1-800-237-9932

Contents

Gorilla

Gorillas are closely related to humans. They are mammals like us. Like all mammals (with the exception of rare, egg-laying mammals), they give birth to live young and feed them milk. A baby gorilla stays with its mother for three years before it starts sleeping in its own nest. Gorillas live in jungles in Africa. They eat plants and sometimes insects.

Gorillas live in troops which are led by a big ***silverback*** *male. The young are often carried around on their mother's back when they travel to feeding grounds.*

Inside a Gorilla

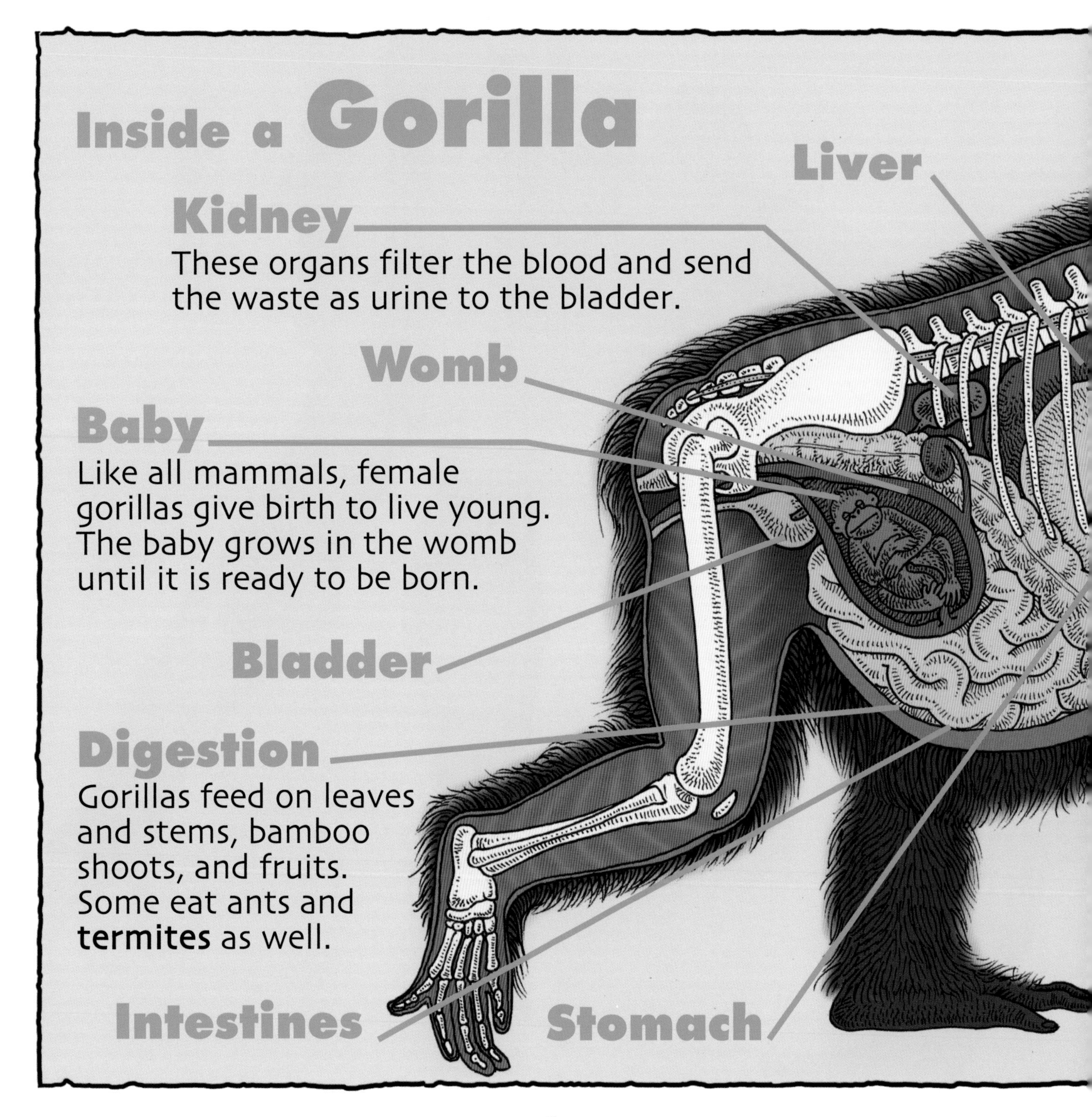

Kidney
These organs filter the blood and send the waste as urine to the bladder.

Baby
Like all mammals, female gorillas give birth to live young. The baby grows in the womb until it is ready to be born.

Digestion
Gorillas feed on leaves and stems, bamboo shoots, and fruits. Some eat ants and **termites** as well.

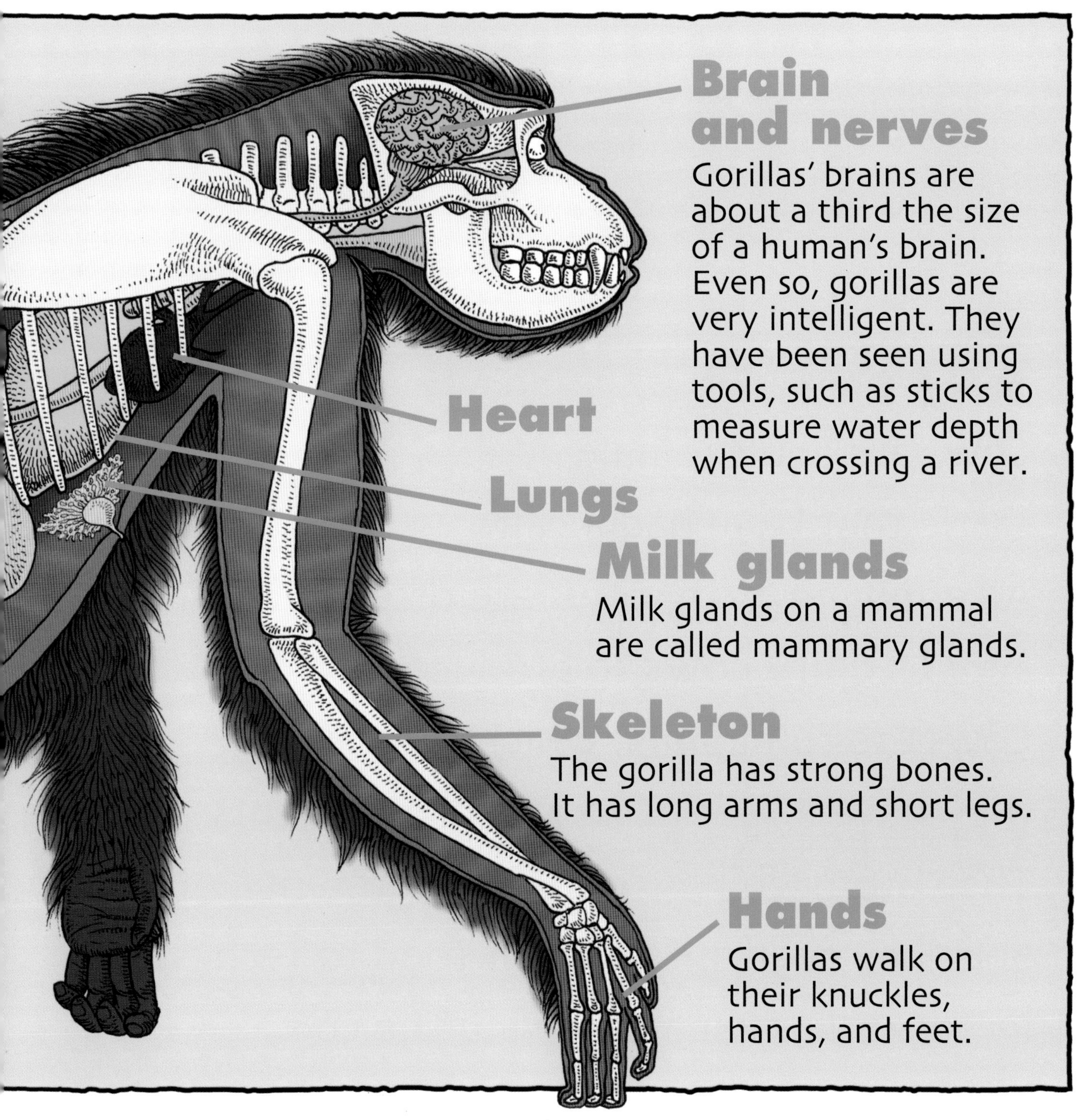

Brain and nerves

Gorillas' brains are about a third the size of a human's brain. Even so, gorillas are very intelligent. They have been seen using tools, such as sticks to measure water depth when crossing a river.

Heart

Lungs

Milk glands

Milk glands on a mammal are called mammary glands.

Skeleton

The gorilla has strong bones. It has long arms and short legs.

Hands

Gorillas walk on their knuckles, hands, and feet.

Cow

Cows are adult female cattle that have had a calf. After giving birth, cows are often kept as **dairy cows** to produce milk. Cows are ruminants, which means they have a special way to digest plants. Their stomach has four compartments, and they **regurgitate** their food to rechew it. This is known as chewing the cud.

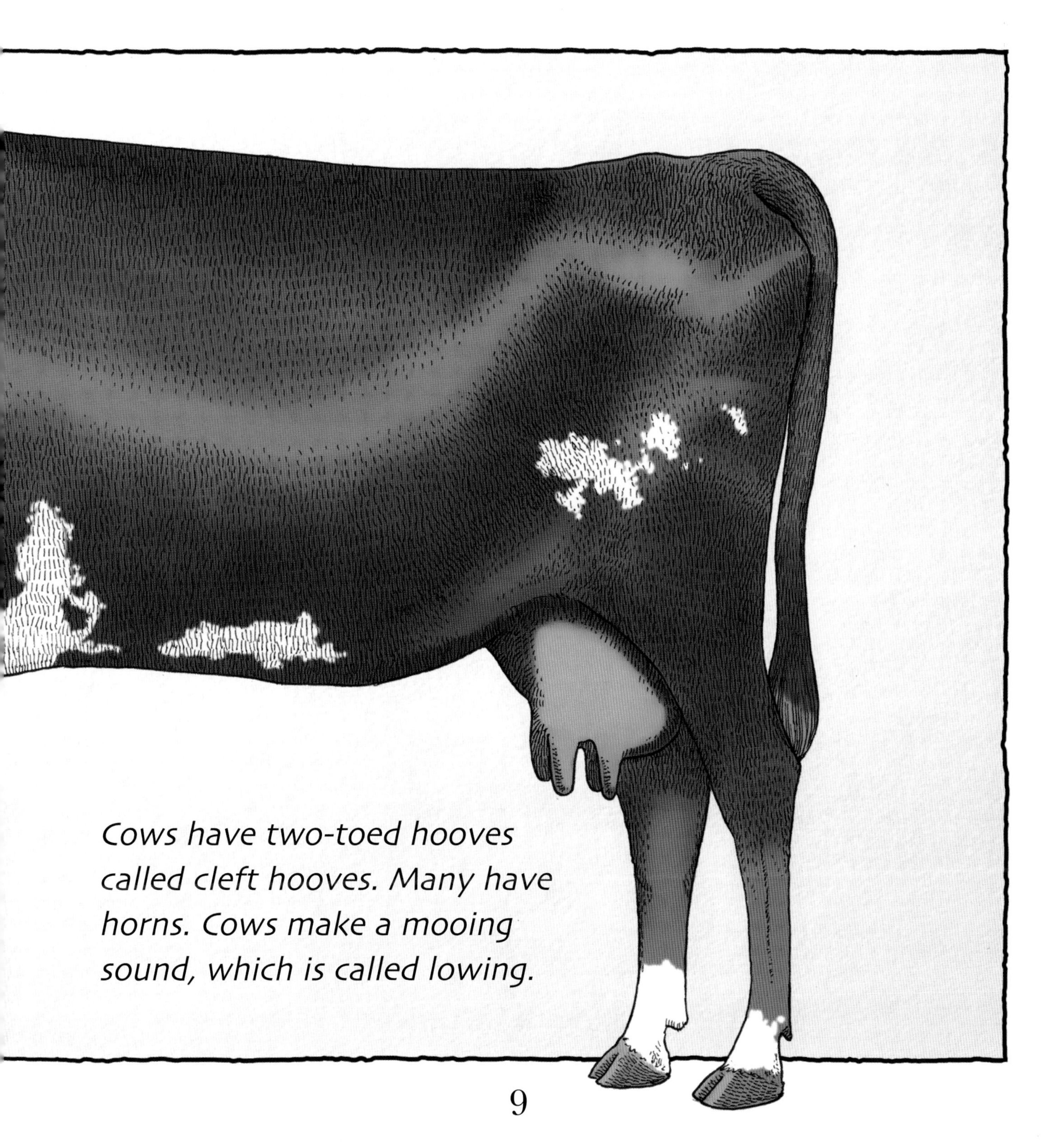

Cows have two-toed hooves called cleft hooves. Many have horns. Cows make a mooing sound, which is called lowing.

Inside a Cow

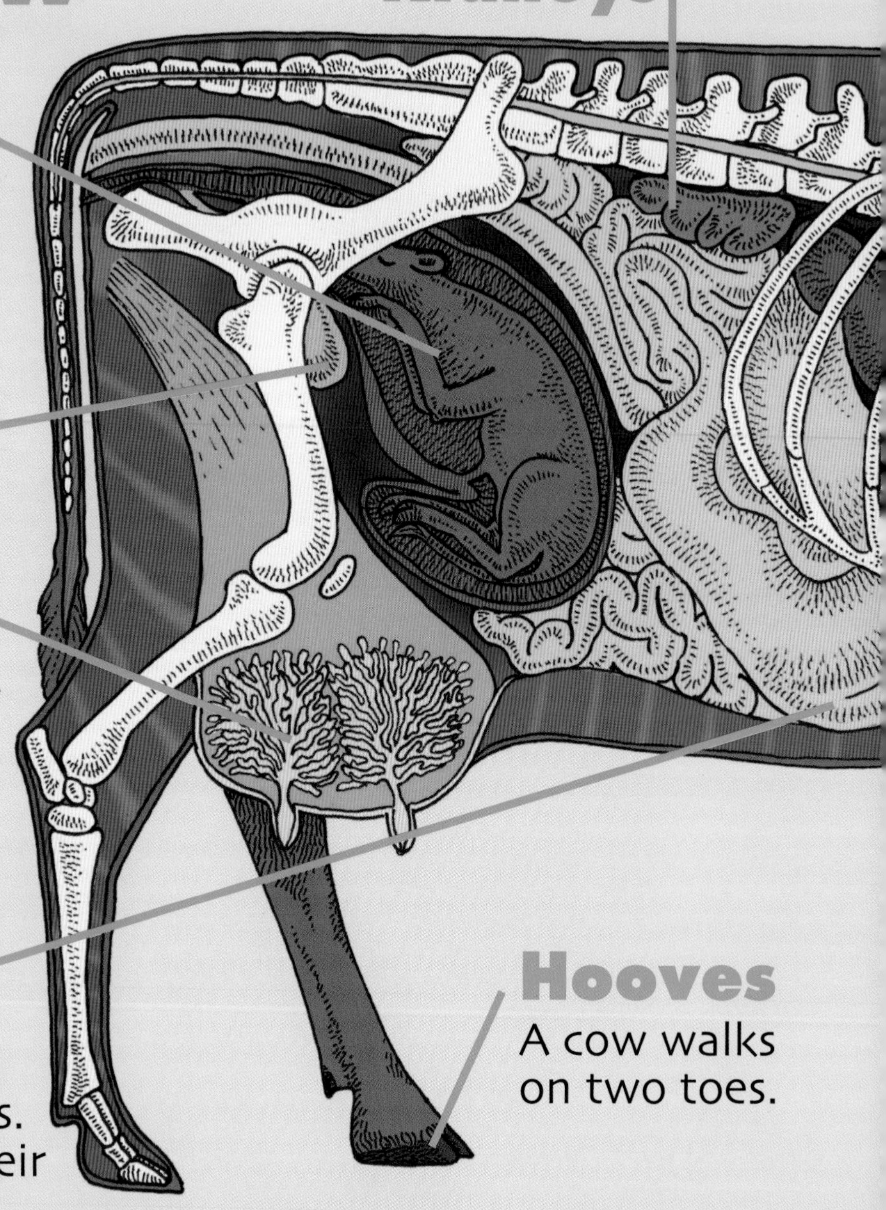

Kidneys

Calf

A baby cow is called a calf. The calf takes nine months to develop before it is born.

Bladder

Milk glands

Cows feed their young with milk from the four milk glands in their udders until the calves are old enough to feed on grass.

Stomach

Cows have one stomach with four compartments. They can regurgitate their food and rechew it.

Hooves

A cow walks on two toes.

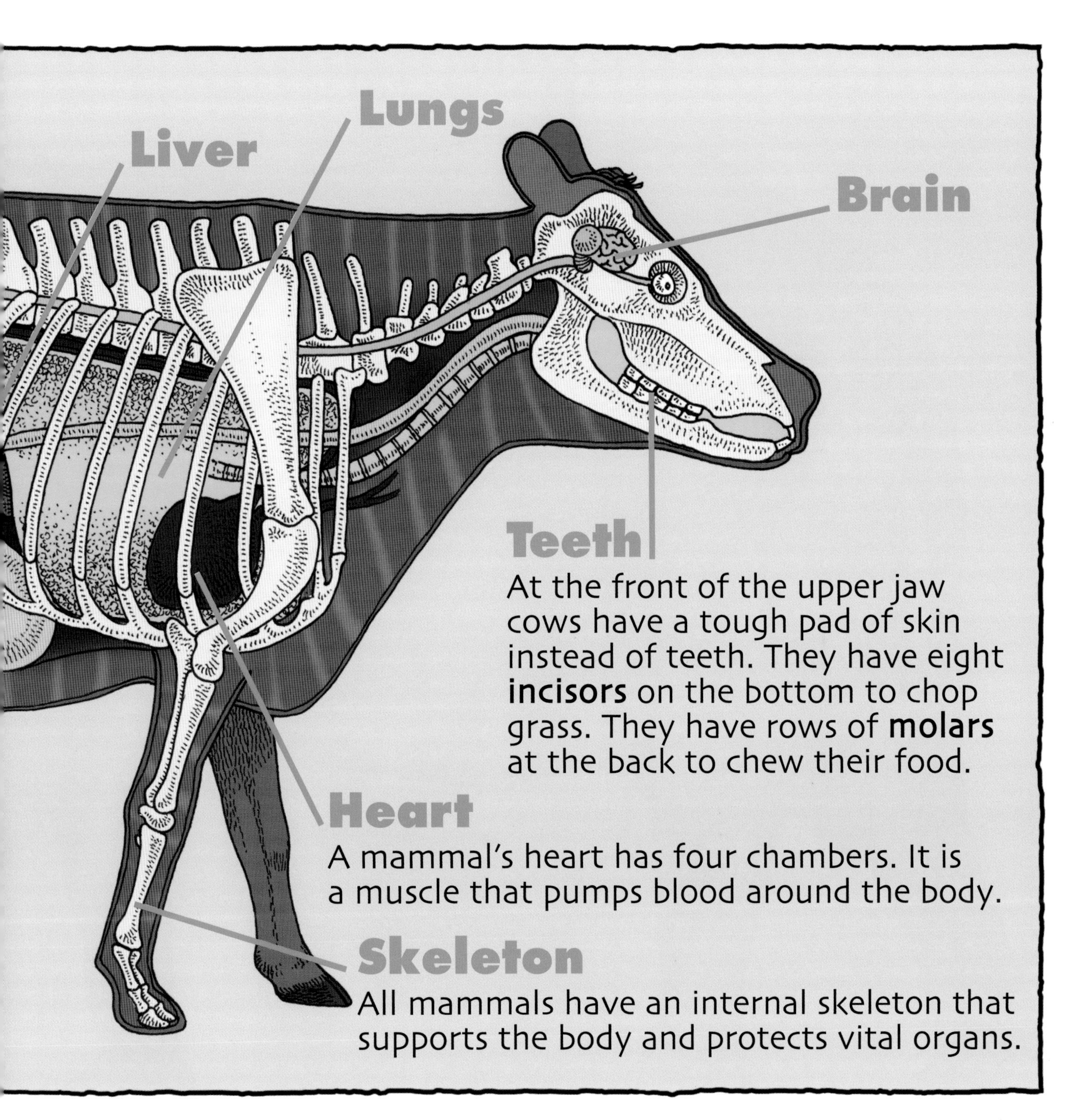
Lungs
Liver
Brain
Teeth
At the front of the upper jaw cows have a tough pad of skin instead of teeth. They have eight **incisors** on the bottom to chop grass. They have rows of **molars** at the back to chew their food.
Heart
A mammal's heart has four chambers. It is a muscle that pumps blood around the body.
Skeleton
All mammals have an internal skeleton that supports the body and protects vital organs.

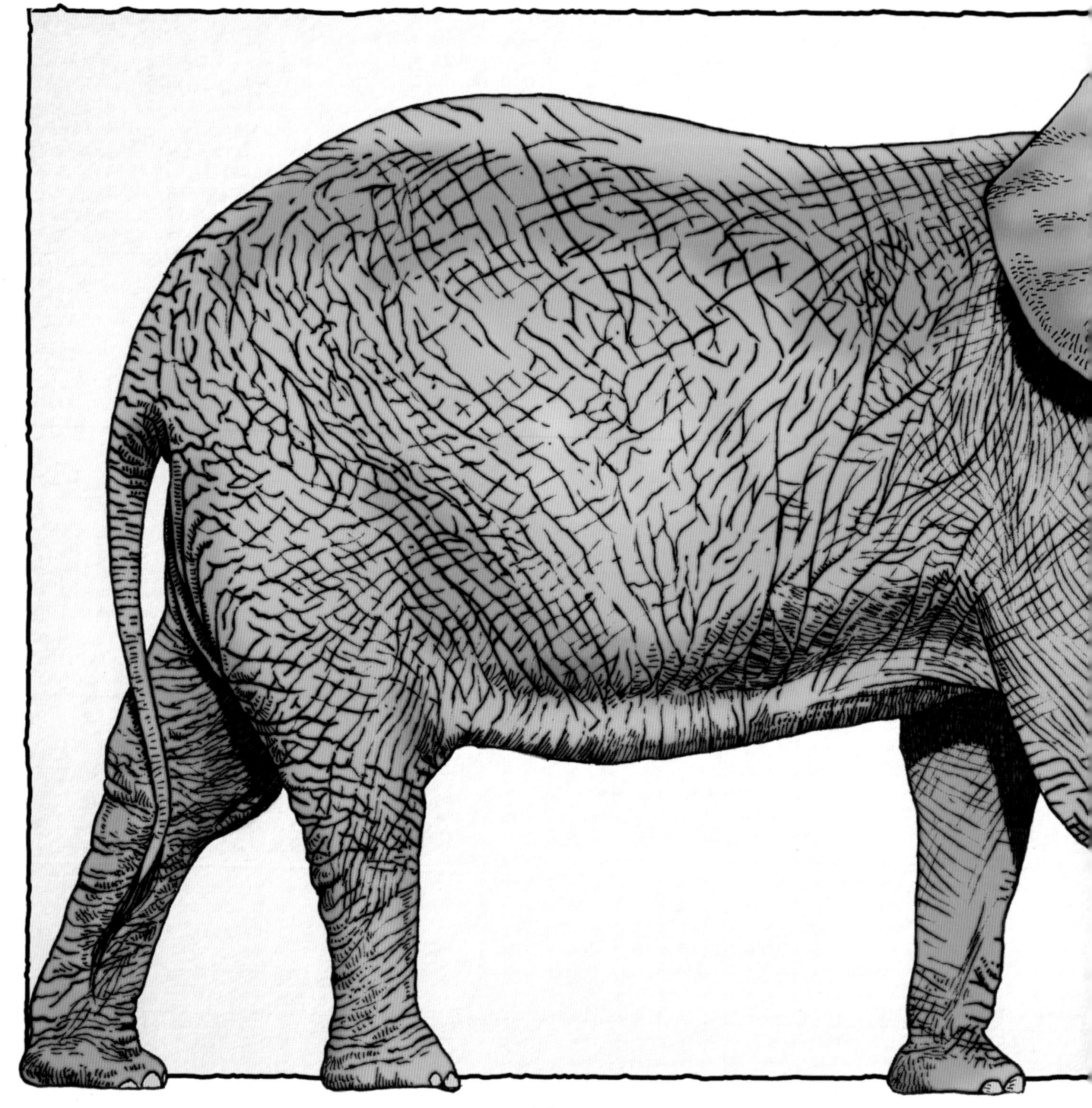

Elephant

Elephants are the largest living land animal. They can reach a height of 13 feet (4 m) and weigh around 7.7 tons (6.9 mt). Their long trunks are used for lifting water and grasping objects. Their large bodies could get overheated, but their ears act like large radiators to keep them cool.

Elephants are very intelligent. They greet each other with their trunks and talk using low rumbles.

Brain

An elephant's brain is four times larger than a human brain.

Skull

The skull contains air holes to make it lighter.

Tusks

These are very long incisor teeth. They use them for digging for food and ripping bark off trees.

Trunk

The trunk has more than 40,000 muscles. It can grasp things and sucks up water to pour into the elephant's mouth.

Milk gland

Elephants have two milk glands which feed their calves for around four years.

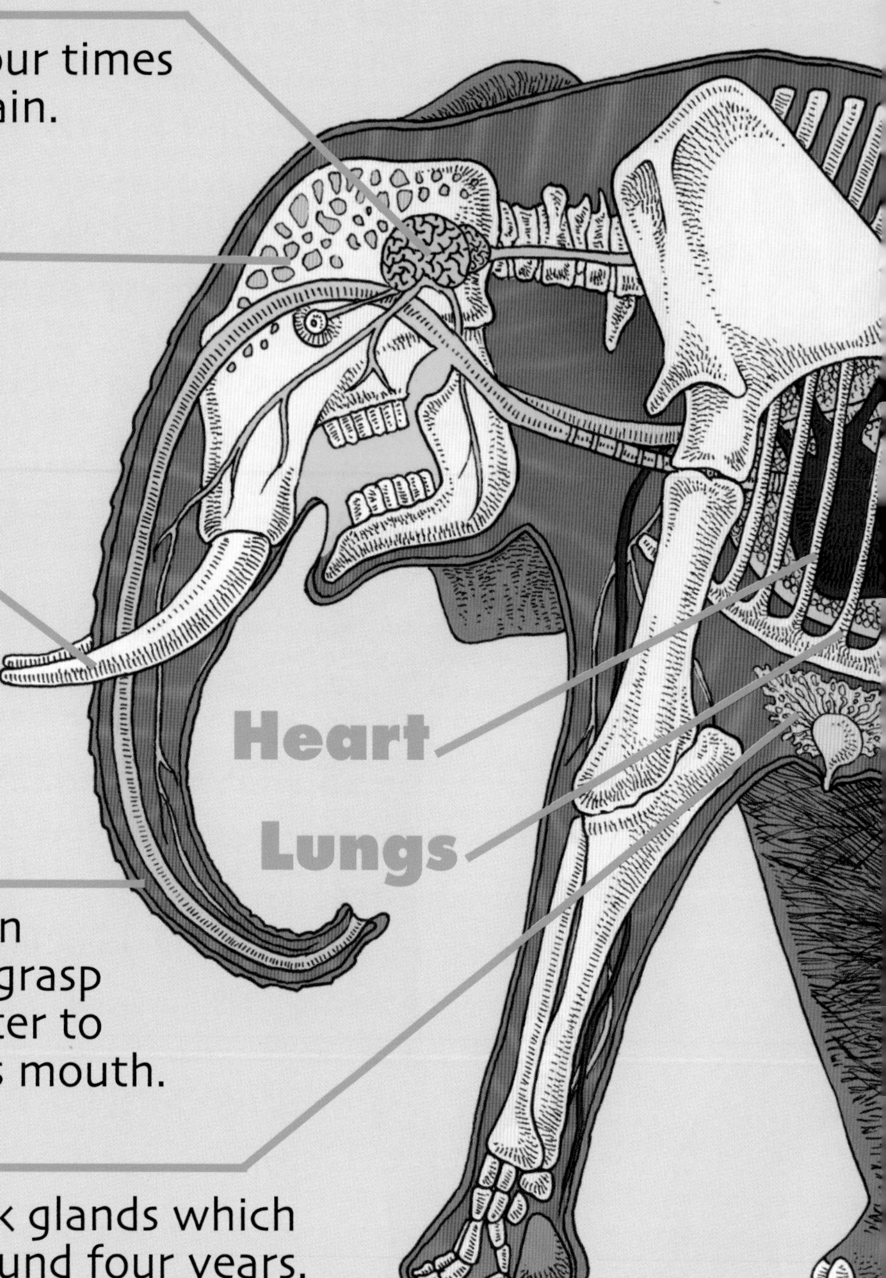

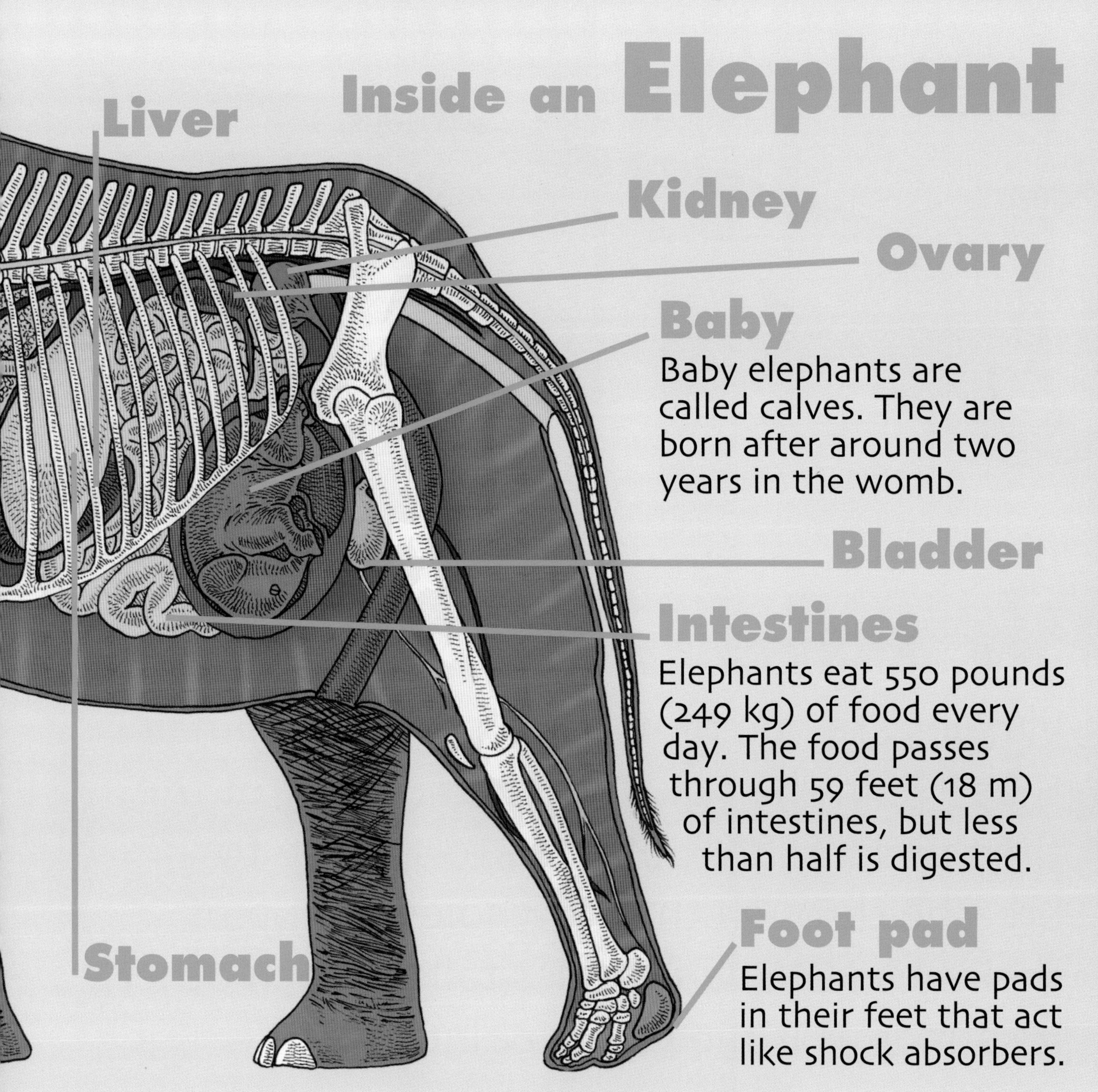
Inside an Elephant
Liver
Kidney
Ovary
Baby
Baby elephants are called calves. They are born after around two years in the womb.
Bladder
Intestines
Elephants eat 550 pounds (249 kg) of food every day. The food passes through 59 feet (18 m) of intestines, but less than half is digested.
Foot pad
Elephants have pads in their feet that act like shock absorbers.
Stomach

Whale

Whales are one of many types of mammals that live in the sea. They spend most of the time underwater but need to surface to breathe through the blowholes on top of their heads. When whales talk to each other, it sounds as if they are singing.

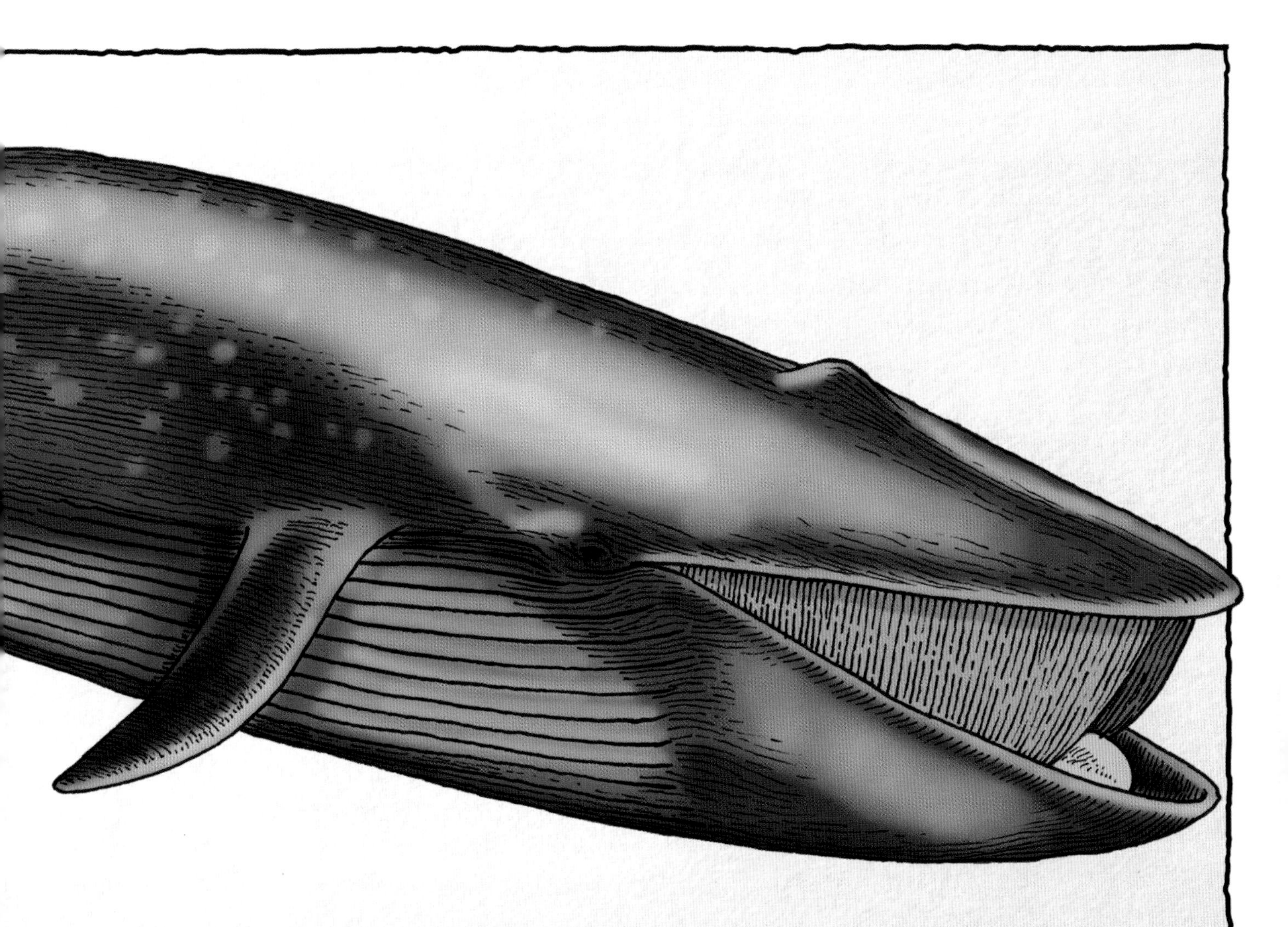

This is a blue whale. It is the largest animal on Earth. Blue whales can grow up to 98 feet (30 m) in length and weigh as much as 191 tons (173 mt). That's the same weight as 25 African elephants!

Inside a Whale

Tail

The whale's enormous tail is made up of two flukes. It uses its tail to plow through the ocean and to make deep dives of around 650 feet (198 m).

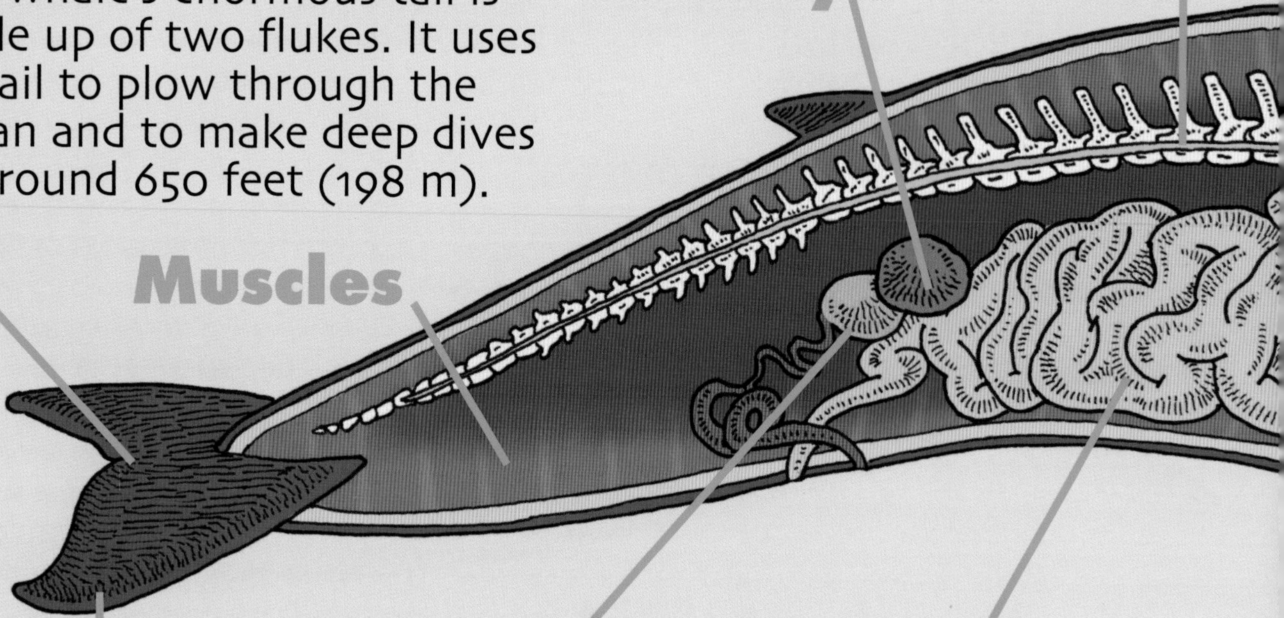

Skeleton

Kidney

Muscles

Fluke

Bladder

Intestines

After the stomach, the intestines break down the food even further. They need to work hard because a blue whale can eat more than 3.9 tons (3.5 mt) of food a day.

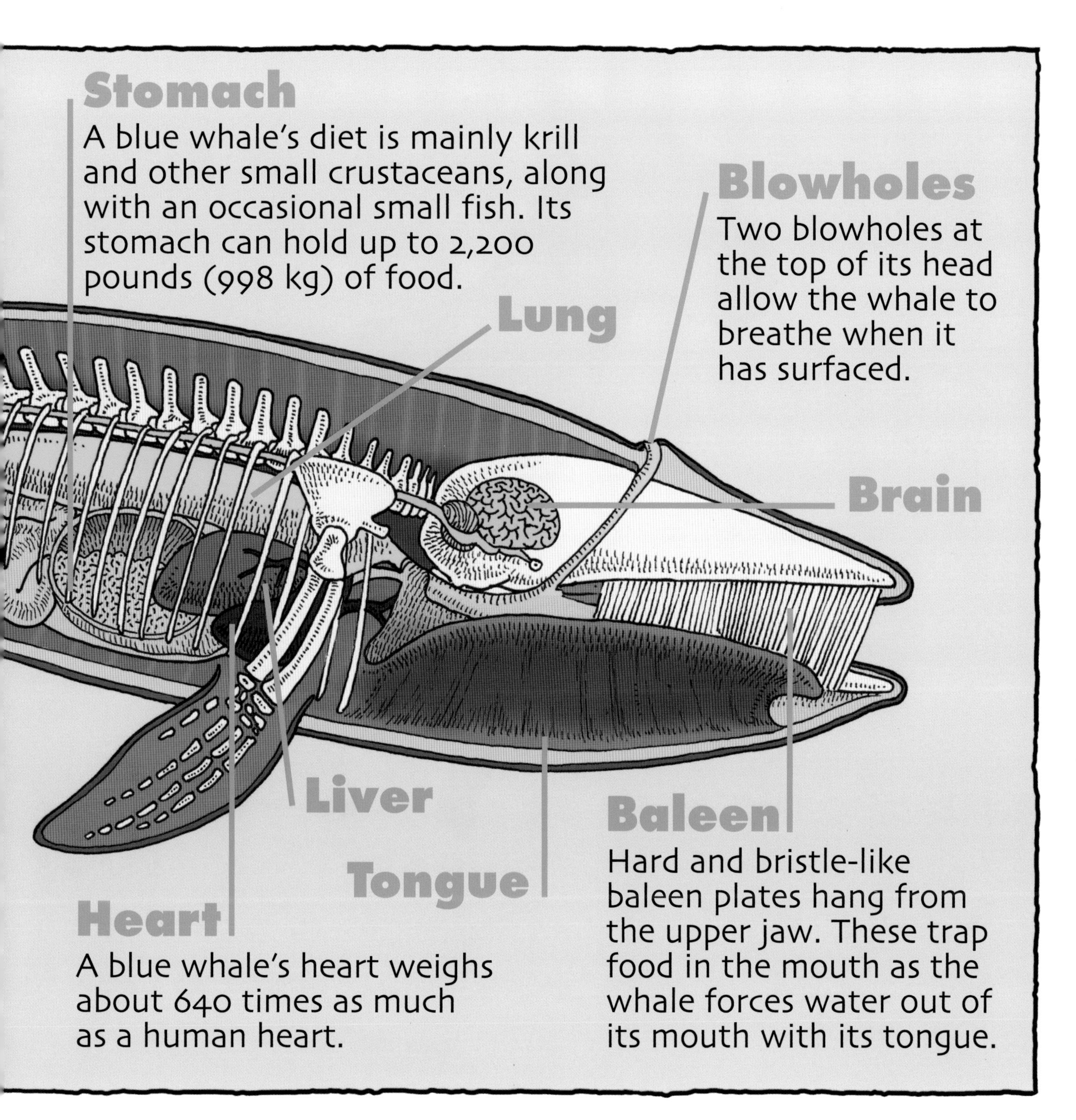
Stomach
A blue whale's diet is mainly krill and other small crustaceans, along with an occasional small fish. Its stomach can hold up to 2,200 pounds (998 kg) of food.
Blowholes
Two blowholes at the top of its head allow the whale to breathe when it has surfaced.
Lung
Brain
Liver
Baleen
Tongue
Hard and bristle-like baleen plates hang from the upper jaw. These trap food in the mouth as the whale forces water out of its mouth with its tongue.
Heart
A blue whale's heart weighs about 640 times as much as a human heart.

Kangaroo

Kangaroos are marsupials. Marsupials are a type of mammal that carry their babies around in a pouch. Kangaroos live in Australia. They live in groups called mobs. They have powerful back legs, which they hop around on, and a long muscular tail for balance. Like cows, they regurgitate the vegetation they have eaten, chew it as cud, and then swallow it again.

A kangaroo's baby is called a joey. At a few weeks old, the joey can leave the pouch for short periods of time. It continues to use the pouch for up to a year.

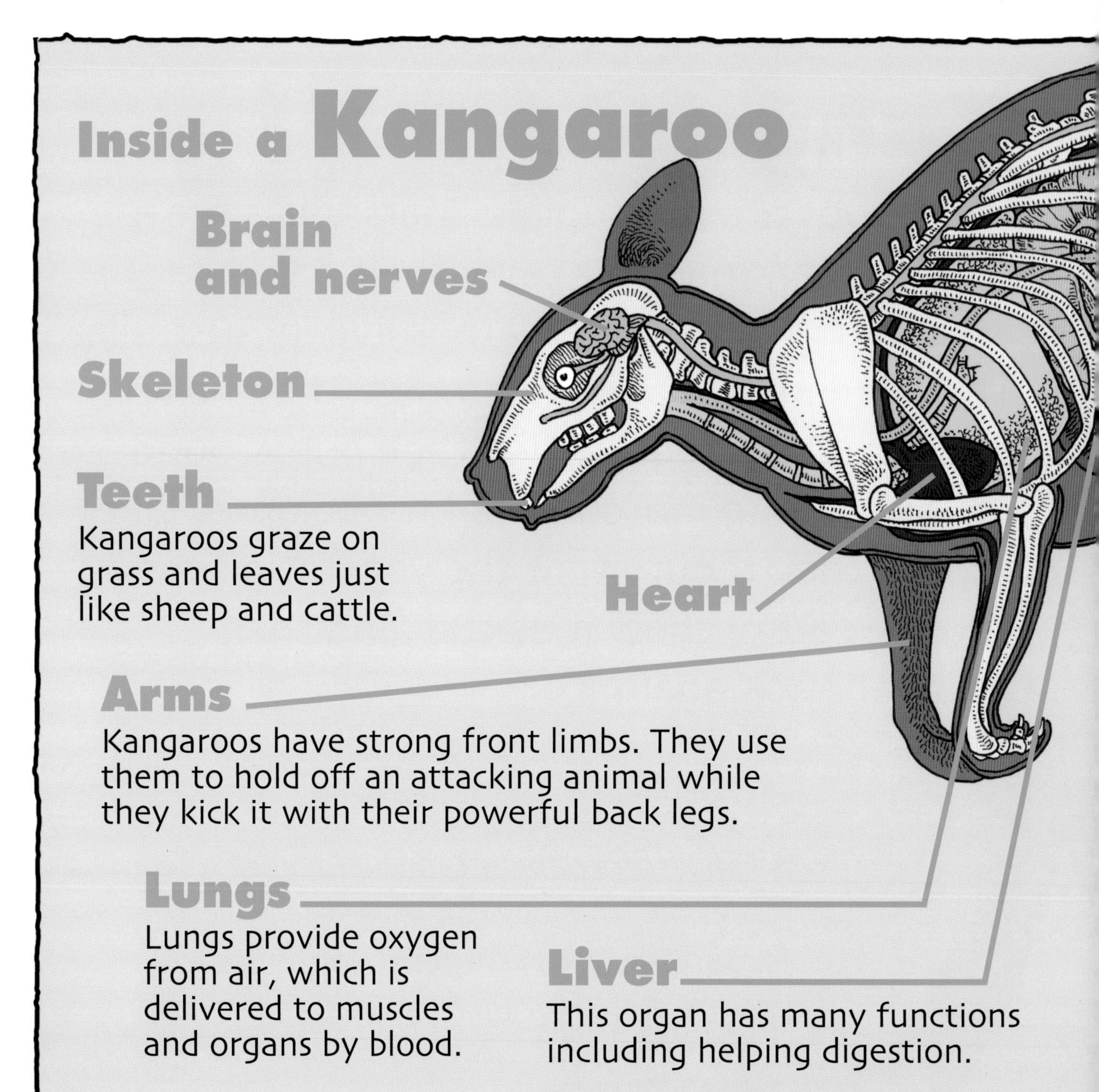
Inside a Kangaroo
Brain and nerves
Skeleton
Teeth
Kangaroos graze on grass and leaves just like sheep and cattle.
Heart
Arms
Kangaroos have strong front limbs. They use them to hold off an attacking animal while they kick it with their powerful back legs.
Lungs
Lungs provide oxygen from air, which is delivered to muscles and organs by blood.
Liver
This organ has many functions including helping digestion.

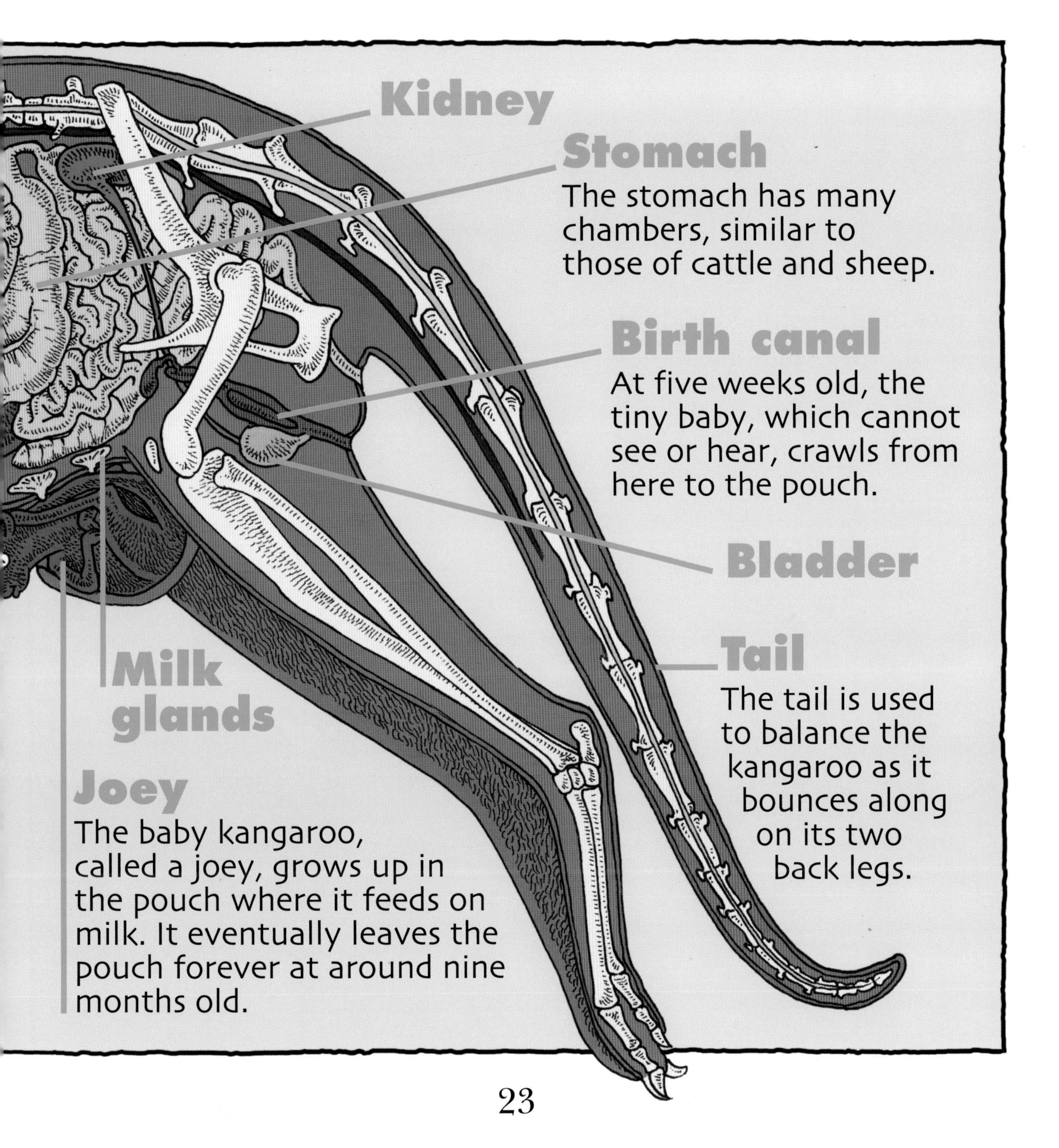
Kidney
Stomach
The stomach has many chambers, similar to those of cattle and sheep.
Birth canal
At five weeks old, the tiny baby, which cannot see or hear, crawls from here to the pouch.
Bladder
Tail
The tail is used to balance the kangaroo as it bounces along on its two back legs.
Milk glands
Joey
The baby kangaroo, called a joey, grows up in the pouch where it feeds on milk. It eventually leaves the pouch forever at around nine months old.

Glossary

dairy cow A cow that is kept by humans for its milk.

incisors Thin-edged teeth at the front of a mammal's mouth.

molars Grinding teeth at the back of a mammal's mouth.

regurgitate Bring swallowed food back up to the mouth.

silverback An adult male gorilla that has an area of white or silvery hair across its back.

termite A small, pale, soft-bodied insect that lives in large numbers in nests made of earth.

Index